My Mum

A child's-eye view
in words and pictures

EDITED BY

Emma Forbes

IN ASSOCIATION WITH
BABY LIFELINE

Hodder & Stoughton

First published in 1997 by Hodder & Stoughton
A division of Hodder Headline PLC

10 9 8 7 6 5 4 3 2 1

British Library Cataloguing in Publication Data

ISBN: 0 340 68946 3

Printed and bound in Great Britain by
Butler & Tanner Ltd, Frome, Somerset

Hodder and Stoughton
A division of Hodder Headline PLC
338 Euston Road
London NW1 3BH

Foreword

I would firstly like to say how flattered I was to be asked to write the foreword to this book. I met Judy Ledger, Founder and Chief Executive of Baby Lifeline, in February 1997, when she came to be interviewed on a radio show I was hosting in London. Upon hearing her story of losing three premature babies and learning of her dedication in building the charity Baby Lifeline, which has saved thousands of lives throughout the UK, I felt compelled to get involved.

My Mum is the most wonderful celebration of motherhood and all that it entails. This collection of funny, moving and downright silly phrases, poems and anecdotes encapsulates that terribly special relationship between a child and his or her mum. My Mum, Nanette Newman, and I have had such wonderful times over the years and she frequently reminds me of the funny and often outrageous things that I came out with as a child. Even now, I love the wonderfully innocent way in which children always say it like it is!

Over the next sixty pages or so, you will read phrases which will have you in stitches and others which will move you to tears.

I sincerely hope you enjoy *My Mum* and many thanks for supporting Baby Lifeline.

With love and best wishes,

my mum is helpful and kind to me. she is cuddly to me. She plays Bingo.

Hannah, age 7

MY MUM

I love my Mum very much,
Even though she says she's fat,
I don't think she is.

I love my Mum's cooking,
I love the things she buys me,
I like her clothes,
I like the clothes she buys me.

On my Birthday my Mum's so kind,
She gave me money and let me buy anything,
On anyone's Birthday she's kind.

When I said I wanted a hamster for Christmas
I came home and what did I find ....
The hamster I wanted

My Mum's so kind,
My Mum started Weight Watchers,
And now she's on the Flat Stomach Plan,
My Mum goes on the scales nearly every day,
She does all the housework everyday,
She does everything she can do,
I LOVE MY MUM

By Nikita Lobb aged 7

"My mum is very pretty, she has a long neck like a giraffe."

From Hazel Thornton. Aged. 3.

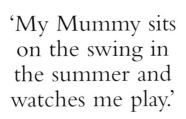

'My Mummy sits
on the swing in
the summer and
watches me play.'

Alicia, age 6,
daughter of Joanne, Countess of Bradford

I love my mummy

From the bottom of my tummy

Siobhan McGovern age 6.

My mum when she is going out with my dad!

Clare Whitmore, age 11

Why I love My mum pippa ♡

My mum ~~one~~ once MADE me a swing ~~with~~ with a small TRee, and some Rope. she ~~dosn't~~ don't have much money But she Gives me lovely Time. she is lovely & Gentle sweet & Kind & the prettiest lady in the world apart from pamela anderson (WHO I fancy!) ps my nannie carole is lovely too!!

Stephen Howard-Curtis, age 8

Your the best mum,
That there has ever been,
No one as good,
And no one as keen.
You sacrafice so much,
So that we can have it all,
And if we need some help,
All we need to do is call.
You cheer us up, when were upset;
You tell us off, when weve done wrong,
You put up with our tantrums and sulks,
And help us to grow big and strong.
You've given us unconditional love,
Ever since day one,
You nurse us whenever we are ill,
And make sure our pains are gone.
We just want you to know,
That we love you dearly too,
And for every thing you've done,
We'd like to say a big
          THANKYOU!

Louise Clark, age 12

'Mum's a maniac because she has big boobies and chocolate buttons.'

Talia Arnold, age 3,
daughter of Eastenders' Debbie Arnold

Whitney Lowe, age 8

My mums great,
She's my mate.
I love her, she loves me,
We're as happy as can be.
She is pretty,
and so witty.
Her hair is brown,
She likes her dressing gown.
Thats the poem of my
mum!
And I know you think she's
toatally fun!

Clare Whitmore, age 11

Daisy Cleall, age 5

My mum is like a special friend
and she is always there,
If any time that I fell down
she'll be there at my care.

When that I feel lonely
I really know I'm not.
My mum has always been there
since I was in a cot.

I'd really hate to lose her
I'd really be upset
I'd ~~wouldn't~~ ~~lose~~ hurt her feelings
not even for a bet.

My mummy's having a baby
she loves coffee and mints.
She also enjous music. she dances
around in a ballerina skirt.

Louise Byfield

4 uears.

my mummy's got lots of hair. she loves beans. and she's got a sore ankle.

Robert Watson

3 years

'I really enjoy our school dinners because they taste exactly like Mummy's cooking at home!'

Samantha Tarrant, age 8,
daughter of Capital Radio DJ Chris Tarrant

Dominique Roberts, age 7

my mummy likes driving
her car she doesn't like eggs
fay Harriman
2½ years

A Note of a Lovely Mum

I love my Mummy because she
is a lot of fun. We have lots of
giggles. My Mummy is the best
because she cooks, buys, shops
a lot, looks after me and cares.
She also loves me. She is the best
mum in the world. She
checks everything. Checks hair
for nits, brushes our teeth and
loves us so much. She arranges so
much for us. She is lovely I love
her. My Mummy also says
the most lovely things, that's why
I love her so much.

Emily Tomlins, age 7

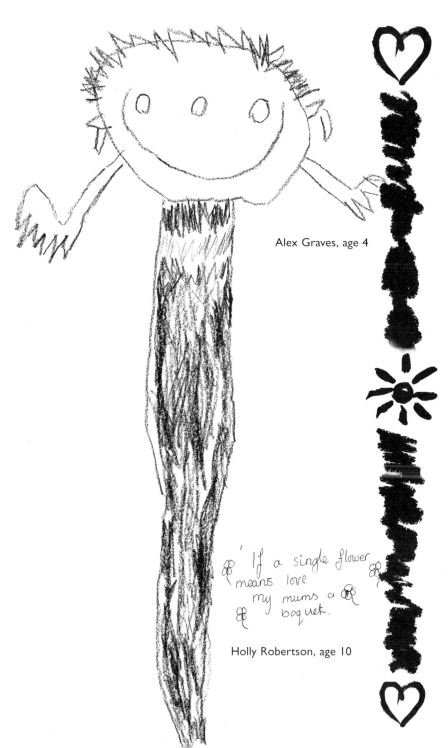

Alex Graves, age 4

'If a single flower
means love
my mums a
boquet.

Holly Robertson, age 10

My mum is cuddly and is nice. And always lets my sister and I have treats. She is fab.

Kristian Philips, age 7

'My Mummy has a big head and body she loves teddy bears.'

Alexander Cowell, age 3

Dominique Roberts, age 7

My Mum is happy.
She gets sad
when I am bad.

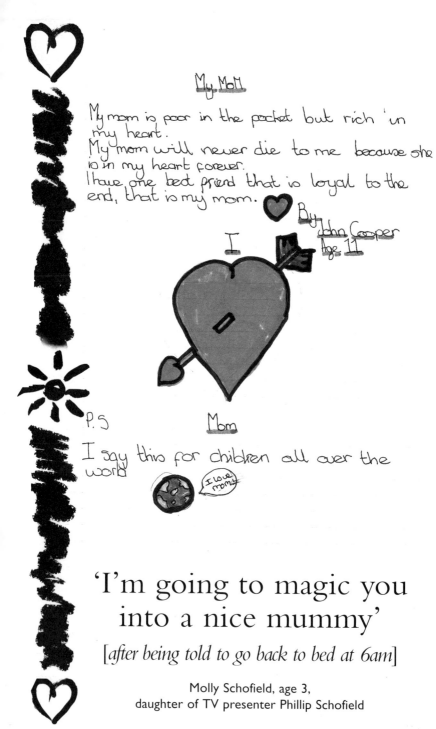

My Mom

My mom is poor in the pocket but rich in my heart.

My mom will never die to me because she is in my heart forever.

I have one best friend that is loyal to the end, that is my mom.

By John Cooper
Age 11

I

Mom

P.S

I say this for children all over the world

I love mom

'I'm going to magic you into a nice mummy'

[after being told to go back to bed at 6am]

Molly Schofield, age 3,
daughter of TV presenter Phillip Schofield

I Love my mum

I Love my mum

from Ben Neale
age 6

I wish i was Big
so that I could marry
my mum and she is nice
and I Love her so so so so
much.

Alexandra Lewis, age 8

My Mum.

My Mum

I think my mum is pretty lovely and kind and cooks me dinner all the time

She never wheres makeup

I Love mamma

Just my

Terri-Anne Winfield, age 8

I Love my mum As well As I love my dog.

Wish she didn't smoke she looks like a frog.

Stevie-Ann Gregory, age 7

IF I DIDN'T HAVE MY MUM WHO WHOULD SHOUT AT ME

MY MUM IS A NO 1 MUM

James Thomas Spain, age 12

I can't tell my mum how much
I love her because there's too many
Reallys.

Sam Ridley, age 8

My mum is kind to me.
My mum wears lipstick and
kisses me on the lips. Oh

Gemma Owen, age 6

my mum is kind to me.
my mum kisses me and everyone
she sees.

Stefania Testa, age 6

When I was 3½
My mum was dyeing the roots of her hair
I said   mummy what are you doing
she said   making myself beautifull
I said   but I like you ugly

Harry Brown, age 10

My Mum

my mum is as cuddly
as a teddybear.
She is as bright as a light
as busy as, a bee, and
She lives with me.

She's as colourful as a
rainbow as caring as a nurse
as happy as a hippo, and she
lives with me.

She's as good as a child
as nice as a friend
She lives with me and I
love her

The end

Cheryl Broad, age 8

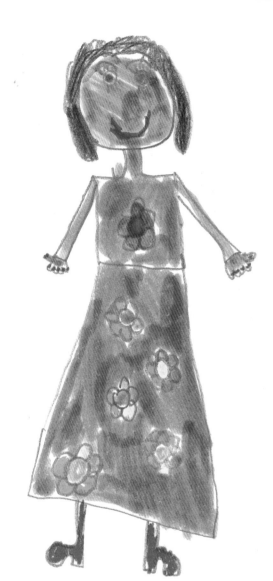

I Love my Mum
my MuM is tall she thinks she is pretty
my Mum Kisses me Some Times

Anna Tiernan, age 7

My mum is cuddly

My mum is kind to me
She is busy at home.
she is nosey.

Lauren Squirrell, age 6

'My Mum is kind to me.
When I am sad she makes me happy.'

Daniel Sheridan, age 6

Emily McKenna, age 4

I think my mum is silly
because she clears up
after me and I make
it a mess again, but
I love her lots and
lots.

Emma sian Bryant
age 7

WHY I Love: mum

Dear Mum

You are a
cleaner upper
bath filler
tucker up into bed
Story reader

Love from

Ryan
x x x x

Ryan James Sheppard, age 6

'I love you, Mummy . . .
I love you, cooker.'

Ben Mayo, age 2½,
son of Radio One DJ and Confessions Host, Simon Mayo

'This is my Mummy.
She is kind and does
lovely cooking.'

Alicia, age 6,
daughter of Joanne, Countess of Bradford

My mum

My mum has brown hair,
And it is all spiked up.
It would be horrible if she
was a witch.

Katie Dove-Dixon, age 6

Sammy-Jo Turner, age 9

MY MULM

Yasmin Khan, age 4½

MY Poem

I love my mum I really do
I just can't say it in the way I do
I know she knows I love her too
but some how that just wont do
So now it comes to an end
and all I have to say to you
is I ♡ You I really do

Sammy-Jo Turner, age 9

'I know about sex, Mummy. And you and Daddy have done it twice.'

Holly Branson, age 7,
daughter of Richard Branson

'My Mummy has got a baby in her tummy and it pops out in the summer.'

Eleanor Barton-Mather, age 4

Sarah McCarron, age 6

my mum is tall
my mum is cuddly
she drinks lots.

Jessica Smith, age 3½

PRETTY GIRL

I ask my mum
to Suck my finger
then tell her
that I have
picked my nose
with it.

jaime
mcginley-Sutton
age 5 years.

Rebecca McKenna, age 7

My Mummy.
I love my mumy because she looks after me and my daddy and my little sister Emily. My mummy is a nurse. She works in the childrens Ward. The picture is of my mummy in her uniform for work. My Mummy is called Debog Mckenna. I love my mum very much.

Rebecca McKenna, age 7

'This picture is of me and my mum. She is juggling and skateboarding.'

Matthew Lungley, age 6

Natasha Deakin, age 6

'I love my mummy
because she cooks
my tea.'

Thomas Lewis, age 6

'My Mummy loves strawberries in actual fact she likes everything, every food and every programme. My Mummy has got big circle eyes.'

Scott Gibbs, age 3

'My Mummy's baby is making a hole in her clothes.'

Kathryn Bates, age 4

I feel my mum
is the grooviest
mum in the
world and she
cares for me.

My mum so lovely
and curly headed

Amy McGrath, age 9½

I love my mummy because she cares for me. She cooks for me and buys me toys. I think my mummy is the best mummy in the world.

age 6
oliver rawlins

My mummy puts my dads clothes on.

Amrik Soar, age 4

'My Mummy likes watching children's ITV. She loves dancing to the Spice Girls. Her favourite food is chicken nuggets with tomato sauce but she don't like spicy chicken.'

Amber Hammond, age 4

Sara Ledger, age 7

'Mummy is funny and
has a happy face.'

Rosie Smith,
daughter of Lorraine Kelly

'My mummy likes butterflies and lions, she doesn't like camels. For dinner, she loves vegetables not bees or wasps.'

George Stuart, age 3

Grace Grantham, age 4½

I Love my mum.
~~So m~~ She is
~~patey.~~ She nos
I. Love her a
I no she love's m
too.

ages

Ailish McBurnes
y

~~McBurney~~